Dragonfly

Stephanie St. Pierre

Heinemann Library
Chicago, Illinois

Designed by Wilkinson Design
Illustration by David Westerfield
Printed and bound in Hong Kong

06 05 04 03 02
10 9 8 7 6 5 4 3 2 1

Library of Congress Cataloging-in-Publication Data
St. Pierre, Stephanie.
     Dragonfly / Stephanie St. Pierre.
        p. cm. -- (Bug books)
     Includes bibliographical references.
     ISBN 1-58810-171-1 (lib. bdg.)
        1. Dragonflies--Juvenile literature. [1. Dragonflies.] I. Title. II.
Series.
     QL520 .S74 2001
     595.7'33--dc21
     00-011429

Acknowledgments
The author and publishers are grateful to the following for permission to reproduce copyright material:
Cover: Stephen Dalton/Animals Animals
pp. 4, 18 Animals Animals; p. 5 Maria Zorn/Animals Animals; p. 6 Gary Meszaros/Photo Researchers; p. 7
Kim Taylor/Bruce Coleman, Inc.; pp. 8, 16, 25 Stephan Dalton/Animals Animals; p. 9 Kim Taylor/Bruce
Coleman, Inc.; p. 10 Hans Pfletschinger/Peter Arnold, Inc.; p. 11 G. I. Bernard/Oxford Scientific Films; p. 12
E. R. Degginger/Photo Researchers, Inc.; p. 13 FLY D. NYM/Photo Researchers, Inc.; p. 14 Stephan
Dalton/Photo Researchers, Inc.; p. 15 Dwight Kuhn; p. 17 Lynn M. Stone/Animals Animals; p. 19 Joe
McDonald/Animals Animals; p. 20 Gary Meszaros/Bruce Coleman, Inc.; p. 21 Robert Armstrong/Animals
Animals; p. 22 Bill Beatty/Animals Animals; p. 23 Kenneth H. Thomas/Photo Researchers, Inc.; p. 24
Robert Lubeck/Animals Animals; p. 26 Corbis; p. 27 Joan Cancalosi/Peter Arnold, Inc.; p. 28 John
Gerlach/Animals Animals; p. 29 Rhoda Sidney/Photo Edit.
Special thanks to James Rowan, for his help in the preparation of this book.

Every effort has been made to contact copyright holders of any material reproduced in this book. Any
omissions will be rectified in subsequent printings if notice is given to the publisher.

Some words are shown in bold, **like this**. You can find out what they mean by
looking in the glossary.

Contents

What Are Dragonflies?. 4

What Do Dragonflies Look Like? 6

How Are Dragonflies Born?. 8

How Do Dragonflies Grow? 10

How Do Dragonflies Change?. 12

What Do Dragonflies Eat?. 14

Where Do Dragonflies Live? 16

What Do Dragonflies Do?. 18

How Do Dragonflies Move?. 20

How Long Do Dragonflies Live? 22

Which Animals Attack Dragonflies? . . 24

How Are Dragonflies Special? 26

Thinking about Dragonflies 28

Bug Map. 30

Glossary. 31

More Books to Read 32

Index 32

What Are Dragonflies?

Dragonflies are **insects.** There are over 500 different kinds of dragonflies in North America. They get their name because they look fierce, like little dragons.

Dragonflies are not fierce. They do not bite people. They do not harm plants or animals. They do not carry any disease.

What Do Dragonflies Look Like?

Dragonflies are colored green, blue, or red. They have long, thin bodies. They have two pairs of long wings. Some dragonflies are so big their wings stretch wider than a person's hand. Most dragonflies are the size of your finger.

Dragonflies have a mouth with sharp **jaws** for grabbing and eating other bugs. They have two big eyes and two small **antennae.** They have three pairs of legs.

How Are Dragonflies Born?

Dragonflies lay eggs. Some lay their eggs in the water. Other dragonflies lay eggs into the stems of plants that grow near the water. When the eggs **hatch,** the young will live in the water.

The eggs hatch after about four weeks. The young are called **nymphs.** They are about the size of a person's eyelash. They do not have wings.

How Do Dragonflies Grow?

Dragonfly **nymphs** have a special **jaw** that shoots far out from their mouth to grab **prey.** They eat lots of mosquito **larvae** to help them grow.

The nymphs grow too big for their skin and shed it. This is called **molting.** The nymphs molt many times before they reach adult size.

How Do Dragonflies Change?

Finally the **nymph** is ready to change into an adult. It climbs out of the water and up a stem, and hangs on tight with its claws.

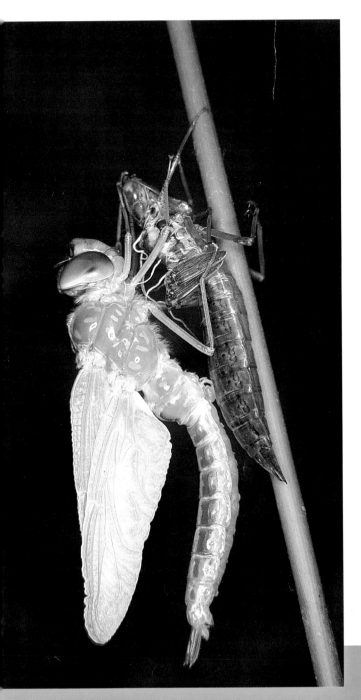

The nymph rests for a little while. Then it breaks out of its old skin for the last time. It rests again while its body gets dry and hard.

What Do Dragonflies Eat?

Dragonfly **nymphs** are **predators.** They hunt and eat tadpoles, small frogs, and the **larvae** of other **insects.** They even eat small fish and **crustaceans.**

Adult dragonflies hunt while they fly. Their good eyesight helps them see other flying insects. They may hunt in groups to feed on large groups of smaller insects, like mosquitoes.

Where Do Dragonflies Live?

There are dragonflies in every part of the world where there is water. They live near streams, ponds, lakes, rivers, marshes, and even waterfalls.

Before they have wings, dragonflies spend most of their lives in the water. When they fly they may travel miles away from water.

What Do Dragonflies Do?

Dragonfly **nymphs** live in water. They swim around water plants. They sometimes lie flat at the bottom of a pond or lake.

Adult dragonflies fly. They can zip up and down, turn, and stop in an instant. They can even fly backwards. They are also strong. They can lift things much heavier than they are.

How Do Dragonflies Move?

The **nymphs** breathe through **gills** inside their bodies. They move by shooting water through their gills. They can move faster than most creatures that live in the water.

Dragonflies use two sets of wings to fly. Before it can fly, the dragonfly must shake and shiver to warm up its wings. The movement of its wings during flight keeps the dragonfly warm.

How Long Do Dragonflies Live?

Most dragonflies in North America will live for a few years as **nymphs** in the water. The rest of the dragonfly's life is usually only a few months long.

The most dangerous time in a dragonfly's life is just after **molting.** It cannot fly or defend itself until its new wings and body dry and harden.

Which Animals Attack Dragonflies?

Birds and frogs eat dragonflies if they can catch them. They catch the dragonflies when they are laying eggs, or when they are **molting.**

Dragonflies are fast fliers. They can fly a lot faster than a person can run. Most of the time the dragonfly is too fast to be caught and eaten by birds or frogs.

How Are Dragonflies Special?

Dragonflies are amazing fliers. They can perform tricks in the air that even helicopters can't copy.

Dragonflies have been around for millions of years. **Fossils** have been found that prove dragonflies are even older than dinosaurs. Those dragonflies were as big as owls.

Thinking about Dragonflies

What must a dragonfly do before it is ready to fly? Why do dragonflies shiver?

This child wants to catch a dragonfly. Do you think it will be easy or hard? Why?

Bug Map

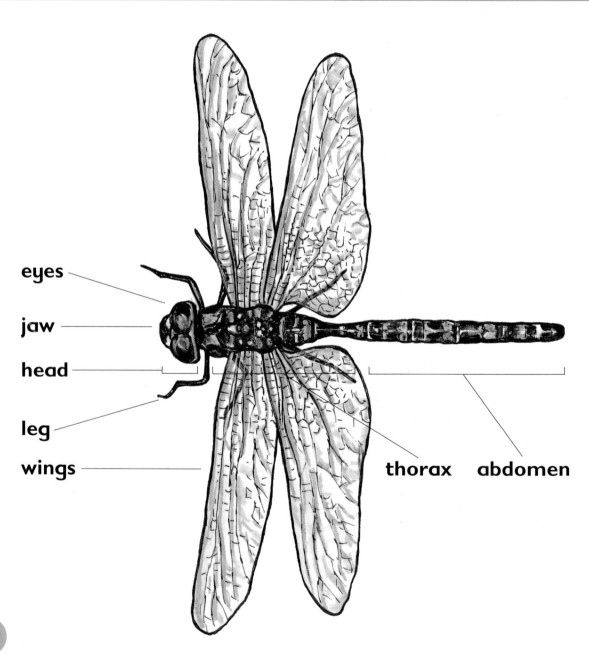

eyes

jaw

head

leg

wings

thorax   abdomen

Glossary

abdomen tail end of an insect

antenna (more than one are called antennae) long, thin tube that sticks out from the head of an **insect**. Antennae can be used to smell, feel, hear, or sense direction.

crustacean relative of insects that has a tough shell, including pillbugs, sowbugs, shrimp, lobsters, and barnacles

fossil picture left in stone of animals that lived a long time ago

gill part of the body that takes air out of water so that fish can breathe in the water

hatch to be born out of an egg

insect small animal with six legs

jaw bony parts that make the shape of the mouth

larva (more than one are called larvae) insect baby that hatches from an egg and does not look like the adult insect

molting shedding the old, outer layer of skin that has been outgrown

nymph insect baby that has hatched from an egg and looks like the adult insect with no wings

predator animal that hunts and eats other animals

prey animal that is hunted for food

thorax middle part of an insect's body, where the legs are

More Books to Read

Amery, Heather. *Dragonflies*. Milwaukee, Wisc.: Gareth Stevens, Inc., 1996.

Bernhard, Emery. *Dragonfly*. New York: Holiday House, Inc., 1993.

Coughlan, Cheryl. *Dragonflies*. Danbury, Conn.: Children's Press, 1999.

Index

adult 12, 15, 19

appearance 4, 6–7

dangers 23, 24, 25

eggs 8, 9, 24

food 10, 14–15

growing 10–11, 13

habitat 16–17

life span 22–23

molting 11, 13, 23, 24

movement 20–21, 25, 26

nymph 9, 10, 11, 12, 13, 14, 18, 20, 22